Guide to Ireland 2024: The Most Complete Guide to Ireland | Discover Ancient History, Art, Culture, Food & Hidden Gems of Ireland. Plan an unforgettable Trip.

Table of Contents

Introduction

Are you ready to be transported to a land of ancient wonders, majestic castles, and mouth-watering cuisine? If you're dreaming of wandering through the lush green landscapes of Ireland, immersing yourself in its rich culture and history, then get ready for an adventure like no other. Introducing "Ireland 2024: The Most Complete Guide", a carefully crafted journey through the Emerald Isle that will leave you spellbound. From the vibrant tapestry of Irish art to the tantalizing flavors of its traditional cuisine, you'll discover a world of beauty and wonder that will stay with you forever.

Ireland has been a popular destination for tourists since the 19th century. With its breathtaking landscapes and rich cultural heritage, the country has fascinated travelers from all over the world. Famous writers like W.B. Yeats helped to romanticize Ireland in literature, making it even more attractive to visitors.

In the 20th century, the Irish Tourist Board played a crucial role in promoting the country's attractions, leading to significant growth in the tourism industry. Visitors were drawn not only to the stunning natural scenery but also to the warm hospitality of the Irish people. Over time, Ireland evolved into a multifaceted destination, blending ancient heritage with modern vibrancy.

Today, Ireland is known for its friendly locals, traditional music sessions, and welcoming atmosphere. Visitors can explore ancient castles, such as the iconic Blarney Castle, or visit prehistoric monuments like Newgrange. Ireland's culinary scene has also undergone a renaissance, with a focus on fresh, locally sourced ingredients.

Whether you're exploring the streets of Dublin, admiring the windswept cliffs of Moher, or enjoying the tranquility of the countryside, Ireland offers a unique blend of old-world charm and modern vitality. The country's enchanting landscapes, deep-rooted cultural tapestry, and genuine warmth of its people make it a transformative journey that lingers in the hearts of those who visit.

This guide is more than a collection of travel recommendations; it's a key to unlocking the hidden gems and authentic experiences that make Ireland a truly unforgettable destination. We'll delve into archaeological wonders, explore charming towns, embrace the artistic and cultural heartbeat of the nation, savor the flavors of Irish cuisine, and provide practical tips to ensure your journey is smooth and memorable.

As your companion on this exciting journey through Ireland's enchanting landscapes, vibrant cultures, and rich tapestry of experiences, I offer you a guide infused with the warmth of my firsthand experiences and a profound love for the Emerald Isle.

My journey through Ireland has been more than just a series of adventures. It's been a deep dive into the heart of a country that captivates the soul. I've wandered through its lush greenery, marveled at its rugged coastlines, and shared laughter with its warm-hearted people. To me, Ireland is not just a destination; it's a living, breathing entity with a magical allure that draws you in and holds you close.

I've made connections with the locals, delving into their stories and traditions while savoring the hearty dishes that make Irish cuisine a culinary delight. Every step has been a revelation, and every encounter has added a layer to my understanding of this captivating land. From the bustling streets of Dublin to the windswept cliffs of Moher, my journey has been a personal odyssey, and I invite you to join me in this guide.

In these pages, I share not just practical

tips but the essence of Ireland – its

history, its art, its cuisine, and the

intangible magic that lingers in the air.

Together, let's explore Ireland in a way

that transcends the ordinary, where

every word becomes a bridge connecting

you to the heart and soul of this

remarkable destination.

I am not just your guide; I am a
storyteller, a friend who has walked the
cobbled streets, climbed the ancient
castles, and reveled in the melodies of
traditional Irish music. So, let the magic
of Ireland unfold as we turn the pages of
this guide, and may your own adventure
be as immersive and unforgettable as
the ones I've had the privilege to
experience.

Here's to the journey, the discoveries,
and the enchantment that awaits.
Sláinte!.

Chapter 1:

Archaeological Sites, Castles, and Towns

Ireland is a country with a rich history and captivating folklore. It is home to a variety of archaeological sites, castles, and towns that chronicle its dynamic past. The lush landscapes of Ireland hold remnants of ancient civilizations, providing a glimpse into the island's prehistoric roots. From Neolithic tombs like Newgrange, which features celestial alignments, to medieval strongholds like Trim Castle, Ireland's archaeological sites are portals to bygone eras.

The island is dotted with imposing castles, which stand as stoic witnesses to centuries of conquests and conflicts. Every stone in structures such as Blarney Castle and Rock of Cashel resonates with tales of knights, kings, and legendary figures. Irish towns, like Dublin and Galway, blend modern vibrancy with historical charm, showcasing a seamless fusion of past and present. In this exploration, we will walk you through the enigmatic history woven into Ireland's soil, traversing through time to unravel the mysteries and stories etched in its archaeological sites, castles, and towns.

Archaeological Sites

Ireland boasts of its archaeological sites that serve as captivating testaments to the nation's ancient past. These sites draw history enthusiasts and curious travelers alike. From the awe-inspiring megalithic wonders of Newgrange to the imposing monastic settlement of Glendalough, these sites unfold the narrative of Ireland's evolution across millennia. They serve as immersive time capsules, providing invaluable insights into the island's cultural, religious, and social development. Beyond their historical significance, these sites are unparalleled tourist attractions that offer an enriching experience. They seamlessly blend education with awe and provide an unmissable adventure to truly grasp the essence of Ireland's heritage.

Clonmacnoise

Nestled along the banks of the River
Shannon in County Offaly,
Clonmacnoise is an ancient monastic
site that flourished from the 6th to the
12th century. Founded by St. Ciarán in
544 AD, the site became a center of
learning, religion, and craftsmanship.
Its strategic location facilitated trade

and cultural exchange, turning
Clonmacnoise into one of medieval
Ireland's most important monastic
settlements.

The site is adorned with a collection of
beautifully crafted high crosses, round
towers, and intricate stone carvings. The
Cathedral of St. Ciarán, the largest
church on the site, stands as a testament

to medieval architecture.

Clonmacnoise's cemetery contains numerous gravestones, including those of Irish kings, adding a regal touch to its historical significance.

Clonmacnoise offers a vivid glimpse into Ireland's early monastic life and its contributions to art and education. Visitors can explore the site's remarkable structures while immersing themselves in the tranquility that still envelopes the ancient grounds. The intricate stone carvings and historic atmosphere make Clonmacnoise a must-visit, inviting travelers to connect with Ireland's spiritual and cultural roots.

Glendalough

Glendalough, in the Wicklow Mountains, is a monastic settlement founded by St. Kevin in the 6th century. The name translates to "Valley of the Two Lakes," aptly describing its picturesque location. Over the centuries, Glendalough evolved into a renowned center for learning and spirituality, embodying the essence of early Irish monasticism.

The monastic site is adorned with the
iconic Round Tower, St. Kevin's Church,
and a series of ancient stone crosses.
The Upper and Lower Lakes enhance
Glendalough's natural beauty, providing
a serene backdrop to the historic ruins.
The Gateway and surrounding monastic
structures reveal the architectural
prowess of early medieval Ireland.

Glendalough seamlessly combines stunning natural scenery with rich historical and spiritual significance. The peaceful lakeside setting enhances the contemplative atmosphere, inviting visitors to explore the monastic remains while enjoying the tranquility of the surrounding mountains. The harmony of nature and history at Glendalough creates a unique experience that captures the soul of Ireland's medieval past.

Rock of Cashel

Perched atop a limestone hill in County Tipperary, the Rock of Cashel is a formidable fortress that has witnessed over a thousand years of Irish history. Originally the seat of the Kings of Munster, it later became a significant ecclesiastical center. The iconic buildings on the Rock, such as the Cormac's Chapel and the Round Tower, showcase a blend of Celtic and medieval architecture.

Cormac's Chapel, with its remarkable Romanesque architecture and intricate carvings, stands out as a jewel on the Rock. The Round Tower, dating back to the 12th century, served both as a bell tower and a place of refuge during times of attack. The High Crosses, including the famous Cross of St. Patrick, contribute to the site's religious and historical significance.

The Rock of Cashel is an architectural marvel set against the scenic backdrop of the Tipperary landscape. Its historical layers, from royal stronghold to religious center, make it a captivating destination. Visitors can explore the complex while appreciating the stunning views of the surrounding countryside, making the Rock of Cashel an integral stop for those seeking to unravel Ireland's multifaceted past.

Newgrange

Situated in the Boyne Valley of County Meath, Newgrange is a prehistoric monument dating back to around 3200 BCE, predating Stonehenge and the Egyptian pyramids. This Neolithic passage tomb is renowned for its astronomical alignment, allowing sunlight to illuminate its central chamber during the winter solstice. Newgrange is part of the Brú na Bóinne UNESCO World Heritage Site.

The monument's circular mound, made of white quartz and granite, covers a long passage leading to a central chamber. The entrance stone, adorned with intricate carvings, is a testament to the artistic prowess of its builders. The roof box above the entrance allows sunlight to penetrate the chamber during specific times of the year.

Newgrange is a testament to the advanced knowledge and engineering capabilities of Ireland's ancient inhabitants. Its celestial alignment and the sheer scale of the structure make it a remarkable archaeological marvel. Visitors can witness the solstice phenomenon through a lottery system, providing a rare and awe-inspiring connection to the Neolithic past.

Monasterboice

Located in County Louth, Monasterboice was an important

monastic settlement founded in the 6th century. It flourished as a center for religious and scholarly activities, leaving behind a legacy of remarkable Celtic crosses and a round tower. The site was dedicated to St. Buite, and its name, meaning "Monastery of Buithe," reflects its origins.

Monasterboice is renowned for its high crosses, with the Muiredach's Cross being one of the finest examples of Celtic Christian art. The West Cross and North Cross also feature intricate carvings depicting biblical scenes. The round tower, standing tall at over 28 meters, served both as a lookout point and a protective refuge during times of danger.

Monasterboice is a treasure trove of Celtic artistry and medieval architecture. The finely detailed high crosses showcase the skill of the craftsmen from this era, while the round tower adds a sense of mystery to the site. Visitors can explore the historical and artistic nuances of Monasterboice, gaining insights into Ireland's early Christian heritage.

Skellig Michael

Perched on a rugged island off the coast of County Kerry, Skellig Michael is a UNESCO World Heritage Site renowned for its monastic settlement. Established in the 6th century, the site boasts beehive-shaped stone huts and terraced gardens, showcasing the resilience of early Christian monks who sought isolation and spiritual contemplation.

The monastery's stone structures, perched on steep cliffs, offer breathtaking views of the Atlantic Ocean. The island is also home to a diverse seabird population, including puffins. The challenging ascent and the unique blend of natural beauty and historic significance make Skellig Michael an extraordinary archaeological and ecological gem.

Skellig Michael is a testament to the dedication and resourcefulness of early Christian monks who sought solace in isolation. The sheer isolation of the island, coupled with its stunning landscapes, provides a once-in-a-lifetime experience for those who appreciate history, archaeology, and the beauty of the natural world.

Dun Aengus

Perched dramatically on the edge of a cliff on Inishmore, the largest of the Aran Islands, Dun Aengus is a prehistoric stone fort believed to date back to the Bronze Age. Its construction continued into the Iron Age, making it one of the most iconic and well-preserved examples of ancient Irish defensive architecture.

Dun Aengus consists of three massive stone walls forming semi-circular enclosures. The fort's strategic location provides panoramic views of the Atlantic Ocean. The precise construction of the dry-stone walls, without the use of mortar, adds to the marvel of this ancient fortification.

Dun Aengus offers a window into Ireland's ancient past, allowing visitors to appreciate the engineering ingenuity of its builders. The panoramic views from the fort enhance the experience, making it a must-visit for those intrigued by ancient defensive structures and the rugged beauty of the Aran Islands.

Poulnabrone Dolmen

Situated in the karst landscape of the Burren in County Clare, Poulnabrone Dolmen is a Neolithic portal tomb dating back to around 3800 BCE. The dolmen served as a communal burial site, and the remains of over 20 individuals were discovered during excavations, providing valuable insights into Ireland's early funerary practices.

Poulnabrone Dolmen consists of a large limestone capstone supported by two upright stones, creating a distinctive portal-like structure. The site is surrounded by a circular mound, emphasizing its ritualistic significance. Its stark beauty against the Burren's unique limestone terrain adds to the mystique of this ancient burial monument.

Poulnabrone Dolmen is a remarkable example of Ireland's megalithic heritage. Its simple yet evocative design, set against the backdrop of the Burren, provides a profound connection to the Neolithic people who once inhabited the region. The dolmen's accessibility makes it an easily visited site for those interested in prehistoric burial practices.

Knowth

Part of the Brú na Bóinne UNESCO World Heritage Site, Knowth is a large passage tomb complex in County Meath. Dating back to around 3200 BCE, Knowth is one of the most significant

Neolithic sites in Ireland, featuring a
multitude of decorated stones and
satellite tombs surrounding the central
mound.

Knowth's central mound contains two
passage tombs with intricately decorated
kerbstones. The site boasts the largest
collection of megalithic art in Western
Europe, with over 200 decorated stones
featuring spirals, concentric circles, and

other motifs. The sheer scale and artistic complexity of Knowth showcase the sophistication of Ireland's Neolithic inhabitants.

Knowth is a treasure trove of megalithic art, offering a glimpse into the symbolic and artistic expressions of Ireland's ancient people. The site's sheer archaeological richness, combined with its proximity to Newgrange, makes it a crucial stop for those fascinated by the Neolithic period and the enigmatic artistry of prehistoric Ireland.

Jerpoint Abbey

Located near Thomastown in County Kilkenny, Jerpoint Abbey is a well-preserved Cistercian monastery dating back to the 12th century. Founded in 1180, the abbey thrived as a religious and economic hub until its dissolution in the 16th century. Jerpoint Abbey showcases exquisite medieval architecture and stone carvings.

Jerpoint Abbey's church, cloister, and tower remain remarkably intact. The intricate stone carvings on tombs and cloister arcade depict scenes from daily life, biblical narratives, and medieval iconography. The abbey's serene setting along the River Nore adds to its charm, providing a peaceful atmosphere for exploration.

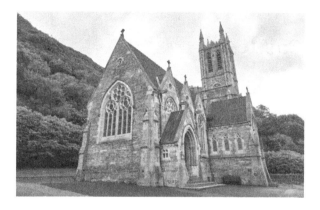

Jerpoint Abbey is a testament to Ireland's medieval Christian heritage, offering visitors a glimpse into the lives of Cistercian monks and the architectural beauty of the period. The finely carved details and the abbey's historical significance make it a delightful stop for those interested in medieval art and the cultural legacy of Ireland's monastic past.

Castles

Ireland's majestic castles are sentinels of its storied past. They tell tales of conquest, royalty, and medieval grandeur. These iconic structures bear the marks of history's passage and are living testaments to Ireland's rich heritage. Irish castles offer a captivating blend of architectural prowess and dramatic landscapes. They are not merely relics but immersive portals into the nation's fascinating history. A visit to these castles is a must-do journey, an opportunity to walk in the footsteps of kings and knights and explore the enchanting layers of Ireland's legacy.

Dunluce Castle

Perched dramatically on the cliffs of County Antrim, Dunluce Castle is a medieval fortress with a tumultuous history dating back to the 13th century. Originally built by Richard de Burgh, the castle has witnessed sieges, battles, and even kitchen collapses into the sea. Abandoned in the 17th century, its haunting ruins have inspired legends and captured the imagination of visitors.

The castle's strategic location offers breathtaking views of the North Atlantic Ocean and the Causeway Coast. The ruins include the iconic Mermaid's Cave and the remnants of medieval chambers. The atmospheric setting and the sea breeze add to the allure of Dunluce Castle.

Dunluce Castle's dramatic setting and intriguing history make it a must-visit. The blend of natural beauty and medieval architecture creates a unique atmosphere, drawing visitors into a captivating tale of resilience and fortitude. Exploring the ruins and taking in the panoramic coastal views ensure an unforgettable experience, making Dunluce Castle a key highlight on any Irish castle tour.

Dunguaire Castle

Located on the shores of Galway Bay in County Galway, Dunguaire Castle is a picturesque 16th-century tower house. Built by the Hynes clan, it later served as a literary and social hub in the early 20th century, hosting renowned figures like W.B. Yeats and George Bernard Shaw. The castle stands as a testament to Ireland's medieval architectural legacy.

Dunguaire Castle's striking appearance against the backdrop of the bay is a photographer's delight. The interior hosts medieval-style banquets during the summer, offering a taste of traditional Irish hospitality. The castle's tower provides panoramic views of the surrounding landscape.

Dunguaire Castle's blend of medieval charm and literary history makes it a unique destination. The opportunity to partake in a medieval banquet adds a festive touch to the visit, allowing guests to step back in time and experience the grandeur of Ireland's past. The castle's strategic location also offers a serene retreat with stunning views of Galway Bay.

Ashford Castle

Ashford Castle is located on the shores of Lough Corrib in County Mayo, It's is a luxurious medieval fortress turned five-star hotel. Originally built in 1228, it passed through various noble families before undergoing extensive renovations. Today, it stands as a symbol of opulence, hosting dignitaries and celebrities in a setting that seamlessly blends history with modern luxury.

Ashford Castle boasts exquisite gardens, a golf course, and a stunning interior adorned with period furniture and artwork. The medieval architecture, including the imposing keep and towers, adds to the castle's regal ambiance. The expansive grounds offer activities such as falconry and boat rides on Lough Corrib.

Ashford Castle is a palatial retreat that invites guests to experience medieval splendor in a contemporary setting. Whether indulging in fine dining, exploring the manicured gardens, or enjoying outdoor pursuits, visitors are immersed in the lap of luxury. Ashford Castle is a testament to Ireland's ability to seamlessly blend its rich history with modern sophistication.

Blarney Castle

Situated near Cork, Blarney Castle is an iconic medieval fortress that has stood since the 13th century. Most renowned for the Blarney Stone, said to bestow the gift of eloquence upon those who kiss it, the castle has a rich history of battles and political intrigue. The stone is set into the castle's battlements, attracting visitors from around the world.

Apart from the Blarney Stone, the castle boasts extensive grounds with gardens, woodland walks, and natural rock formations. The castle's interior showcases medieval architecture, including the Great Hall and battlements. The Poison Garden, featuring toxic plants, adds a touch of botanical intrigue.

Blarney Castle is not just a historic site but an immersive experience. Kissing the Blarney Stone is a tradition that draws visitors seeking the legendary "gift of gab." The expansive grounds offer a peaceful retreat, and the castle's varied attractions cater to a range of interests, making it a versatile and enjoyable destination.

Trim Castle

Dominating the landscape along the River Boyne in County Meath, Trim Castle is the largest Anglo-Norman castle in Ireland. Built in the late 12th century by Hugh de Lacy, the castle played a crucial role in medieval Ireland's military and administrative affairs. Its imposing structure has earned it a place in films such as "Braveheart."

Trim Castle's strategic design includes a central keep, curtain walls, and towers. The Great Hall and various chambers provide insights into medieval castle life.

The surrounding landscape, including the River Boyne and the picturesque town of Trim, enhances the castle's visual appeal.

Trim Castle's sheer scale and historical significance make it a standout destination for castle enthusiasts. Exploring the well-preserved interior and ascending the keep offer panoramic views of the surrounding countryside. The castle's role in cinematic history adds an extra layer of fascination, making Trim Castle a captivating stop for both history buffs and movie enthusiasts.

Malahide Castle

Situated in County Dublin, Malahide

Castle dates back to the 12th century

and has been home to the Talbot family

for over 800 years. The castle

underwent various renovations,

blending medieval and Georgian

architectural elements. Surrounded by

lush gardens and a demesne, Malahide

Castle provides a glimpse into Ireland's aristocratic past.

Malahide Castle's interior showcases period furnishings, impressive portraits, and a collection of historical artifacts. The extensive grounds include the Talbot Botanic Gardens, a butterfly house, and woodland walks. The castle also offers guided tours, providing insights into its rich history.

Malahide Castle combines historical richness with natural beauty, creating a well-rounded visitor experience. The guided tours offer a deep dive into the castle's storied past, while the gardens and surrounding parkland provide a serene escape. Its proximity to Dublin makes Malahide Castle a convenient and delightful day trip for those interested in Ireland's heritage.

Cahir Castle

Strategically positioned on an island in the River Suir in County Tipperary, Cahir Castle is a formidable fortress with roots tracing back to the 13th century. Initially constructed as a defensive stronghold, it evolved over the centuries, witnessing sieges and battles. Cahir

Castle stands as one of Ireland's best-preserved medieval castles, providing a fascinating glimpse into the nation's martial history.

Cahir Castle boasts a well-preserved keep, curtain walls, and a portcullis. The interior includes medieval chambers, a great hall, and a courtyard. The castle's location, surrounded by the river, enhances its defensive features. Guided tours elucidate the castle's historical significance and architectural evolution.

Cahir Castle offers a comprehensive look at medieval military architecture. Its well-maintained structure, strategic location, and informative tours make it an ideal destination for history enthusiasts. The immersive experience of exploring the castle grounds and interiors transports visitors to a bygone era of knights and sieges.

Kilkenny Castle

Located in the heart of Kilkenny City, Kilkenny Castle is a striking example of Norman architecture. Built in the 12th century by the Anglo-Norman Butler family, the castle has undergone various renovations, blending medieval and

Victorian styles. It stands as a testament to the enduring influence of the Anglo-Norman aristocracy in Ireland.

Kilkenny Castle features a central keep, towers, and extensive gardens. The interiors showcase period furniture, artworks, and historical exhibits. The Rose Garden and the restored stables add to the castle's charm. Events and cultural activities are often held on the castle grounds.

Kilkenny Castle combines architectural grandeur with cultural richness. The castle's central location in the charming city of Kilkenny makes it easily accessible. Visitors can explore the well-manicured gardens, delve into the castle's historical exhibits, and enjoy the vibrant atmosphere of this medieval gem.

Bunratty Castle

Situated in County Clare, Bunratty Castle is a well-preserved medieval fortress that traces its origins to the 15th century. Originally built by the MacNamara family, it later became the stronghold of the O'Brien clan. Today, Bunratty Castle stands as a living museum, offering a vivid portrayal of medieval Ireland.

Bunratty Castle features a fully furnished great hall, banquet hall, and a collection of period-appropriate artifacts. The adjacent Folk Park showcases reconstructed traditional

Irish buildings. The castle hosts medieval banquets, providing a delightful blend of history and entertainment.

Bunratty Castle provides a captivating living history experience. The well-preserved interiors, coupled with the immersive Folk Park, transport visitors to medieval Ireland. The option to partake in a medieval banquet adds a festive and interactive element, making Bunratty Castle an engaging destination for all ages.

Ross Castle

Nestled on the shores of Lough Leane in Killarney National Park, Ross Castle is a 15th-century fortress with ties to the O'Donoghue clan. The castle played a role in Ireland's turbulent history, witnessing conflicts and political changes. Today, it stands as a picturesque landmark amid the natural beauty of Killarney.

Ross Castle's distinctive cylindrical towers and battlements overlook the tranquil Lough Leane. The interior features furnished rooms, including the atmospheric Great Hall. The castle's proximity to Killarney's scenic landscapes makes it a popular stop for those exploring the Ring of Kerry.

Ross Castle offers a harmonious blend of history and natural beauty. The serene setting along the lake, combined with the well-preserved interiors, creates a tranquil and captivating atmosphere. Exploring Ross Castle provides a glimpse into Ireland's medieval past amidst the breathtaking landscapes of Killarney.

Charming Towns

Amidst the lush green landscapes of Ireland lie several charming towns that seamlessly blend together history, culture, and undeniable allure. Each of these idyllic settlements has its own unique character, inviting travelers to immerse themselves in a world where cobblestone streets echo with tales of bygone eras, and quaint facades reveal the timeless charm of Irish hospitality. From the coastal gems overlooking the Atlantic to the inland treasures surrounded by rolling hills, Ireland's charming towns embody the essence of the Emerald Isle. Whether adorned with colorful pubs, historic landmarks, or lively markets, these towns invite exploration and promise a delightful journey into the heart of Ireland's warmth and enchantment.

Kinsale, County Cork

Known as the "Gourmet Capital of Ireland," Kinsale in County Cork is a picturesque coastal town renowned for its colorful streets, historic architecture, and culinary delights. The town's scenic harbor, lined with charming shops and eateries, offers a perfect setting for leisurely strolls. Kinsale's rich maritime history is reflected in sites like Charles Fort, while its annual gourmet festival attracts food enthusiasts from around the world.

Dingle, County Kerry

Nestled on the rugged Dingle Peninsula, Dingle town is a vibrant haven with a unique blend of traditional Irish charm and artistic flair. Famous for its resident dolphin, Fungie, the town offers stunning coastal views, lively pubs with traditional music, and a colorful array of shops and galleries. The Slea Head Drive nearby provides breathtaking vistas of the Atlantic and rugged landscapes.

Westport, County Mayo

Surrounded by the captivating landscapes of Clew Bay and Croagh Patrick, Westport is a Georgian gem known for its charming architecture and lively atmosphere. The tree-lined Mall, historic Westport House, and the Great Western Greenway, a scenic cycling route, contribute to the town's allure. Westport's welcoming pubs and vibrant festivals, including the annual Westport

Music and Arts Festival, make it a must-visit destination.

Adare, County Limerick

Adare, often referred to as Ireland's prettiest village, is a captivating blend of thatched cottages, medieval architecture, and immaculately manicured gardens. Adorned with charming streets and the iconic Adare Manor, the town exudes an old-world charm. The Desmond Castle and the Trinitarian Abbey provide glimpses into Adare's rich history.

Kenmare, County Kerry

Nestled at the meeting point of the Iveragh and Beara Peninsulas, Kenmare is a postcard-perfect town boasting a picturesque setting along the Kenmare Bay. The town's colorful houses, charming boutiques, and gourmet restaurants make it a popular stop along the Ring of Kerry. Kenmare is also a gateway to the Beara Peninsula, known for its unspoiled landscapes.

Kilkenny, County Kilkenny

With its medieval streets, iconic castle, and lively cultural scene, Kilkenny is a

town steeped in history and character.
The medieval Kilkenny Castle overlooks
the River Nore, while St. Canice's
Cathedral and the charming Kilkenny
Design Centre showcase the town's rich
heritage. Kilkenny's vibrant arts and
crafts scene, coupled with its traditional
pubs, make it a captivating destination.

Cobh, County Cork

Perched on the shores of Cork Harbour, Cobh is a maritime town with a fascinating history. Known for being the last port of call for the Titanic in 1912, Cobh's waterfront is adorned with colorful houses and historic sites. The Cobh Heritage Centre explores the town's emigration history, and St. Colman's Cathedral stands as an architectural marvel overlooking the harbor.

Clifden, County Galway

Gateway to the rugged beauty of Connemara, Clifden is a vibrant market town set against the backdrop of the Twelve Bens mountain range. Its lively atmosphere, traditional Irish pubs, and annual Connemara Pony Show make Clifden a charming hub. The Sky Road offers panoramic views of the Atlantic, while the nearby Kylemore Abbey adds to the town's allure.

Doolin, County Clare

Situated on the edge of the Burren and overlooking the Cliffs of Moher, Doolin is a small village renowned for its traditional Irish music scene. The town's cozy pubs, such as Gus O'Connor's, are famous for lively sessions. Doolin also serves as a gateway to the Aran Islands, making it a hub for those seeking both cultural and natural exploration.

Ennis, County Clare

Ennis, the capital of County Clare, is a medieval market town with a charming atmosphere. Its narrow streets are adorned with colorful facades, traditional pubs, and historic landmarks such as Ennis Friary. The town's lively sessions of traditional Irish music and the annual Fleadh Cheoil, a renowned Irish music festival, contribute to its cultural vibrancy.

Chapter 3:

Art and Culture

Ireland is a country that is deeply rooted in mysticism and ancient traditions. The country has a rich tapestry of art and culture that has transcended time. From traditional Irish music with its haunting melodies to literary masterpieces, and captivating visual arts, Ireland's cultural landscape reflects the nation's history and resilient spirit. The echoes of folklore and mythology are woven into contemporary expressions, creating a dynamic fusion of past and present. Whether wandering through the halls of renowned art galleries, immersing oneself in the fervor of a traditional céilí dance, or savoring the words of literary giants, Ireland's art and culture are inviting to explore the essence of the Emerald Isle.

Museums and Art Galleries

Ireland's museums and art galleries stand as guardians of the nation's cultural legacy, offering immersive journeys through its rich history and artistic expressions. From ancient artifacts to contemporary masterpieces, these institutions invite visitors to explore the diverse tapestry of Ireland's heritage, fostering a deep appreciation for its art and culture.

The National Museum of Ireland - Archaeology, Dublin:

Located in the heart of Dublin, the National Museum of Ireland - Archaeology is a treasure trove of Ireland's ancient past. The museum houses a remarkable collection of artifacts spanning thousands of years, providing insight into the island's rich archaeological history. Exhibits range from prehistoric Ireland to the Viking and medieval periods. One of the highlights is the collection of bog bodies, remarkably preserved corpses dating back centuries, offering a unique glimpse into the lives of Ireland's ancestors. The Ardagh Chalice and the Tara Brooch, both iconic symbols of Irish craftsmanship, are also on display. The museum serves as a fascinating introduction to Ireland's deep-rooted cultural heritage.

The Irish Museum of Modern Art (IMMA), Dublin:

For those seeking a more contemporary artistic experience, the Irish Museum of Modern Art (IMMA) stands as a beacon of creativity in Dublin. Housed in the stunning Royal Hospital Kilmainham, the museum showcases an impressive collection of modern and contemporary Irish art. From paintings and sculptures to multimedia installations, IMMA embraces a diverse range of artistic expressions. The museum frequently hosts temporary exhibitions, highlighting the dynamic nature of Ireland's contemporary art scene. The beautiful gardens surrounding the museum add to the overall experience, providing a serene backdrop for reflection on the intersection of tradition and innovation in Irish art.

The Chester Beatty, Dublin:
The Chester Beatty is a unique museum that brings together a fascinating array of treasures from around the world. Sir Alfred Chester Beatty, a mining magnate, amassed a remarkable collection of rare manuscripts, prints, and artifacts during his lifetime. The museum's diverse exhibits include illuminated manuscripts, ancient texts from various cultures, and exquisite pieces of Asian and European art. The

Chester Beatty provides a cross-cultural journey, showcasing the interconnectedness of human creativity across different civilizations. Its commitment to education and cultural exchange makes it a must-visit destination for those with an interest in global heritage.

The Crawford Art Gallery, Cork:
Moving beyond the capital city, Cork's Crawford Art Gallery stands as a vibrant hub for the arts in the south of Ireland. Housed in a beautifully restored Georgian building, the gallery boasts an extensive collection of European and

Irish art spanning the 18th century to the present day. The Crawford Art Gallery places a strong emphasis on contemporary Irish artists, providing a platform for emerging talents. The sculpture-filled courtyard adds to the gallery's charm, creating a seamless blend of historic architecture and modern creativity. With a diverse range of exhibitions and a commitment to community engagement, the Crawford Art Gallery contributes significantly to Cork's cultural landscape.

The Ulster Museum, Belfast:

Northern Ireland's premier museum, the Ulster Museum in Belfast, offers a comprehensive exploration of the region's history, art, and natural sciences. The museum's extensive collections cover everything from ancient artifacts and Irish art to interactive science exhibits. Highlights include the Armada Room, featuring items recovered from the Spanish Armada shipwrecks along the Irish coast, and the "Window on Wildlife," showcasing the rich biodiversity of the region. The Ulster Museum provides a holistic cultural experience, blending the artistic and scientific dimensions of Northern Ireland's heritage.

The Hunt Museum, Limerick:

Situated along the scenic River Shannon in Limerick, the Hunt Museum is a hidden gem housing an impressive collection of art and antiquities. The museum, housed in the historic 18th-century Custom House, showcases pieces acquired by the Hunt family. The eclectic collection spans diverse periods and regions, including European and Middle Eastern artifacts, paintings, and sculptures. Notable highlights include works by renowned artists such as Pablo

Picasso and Jack B. Yeats. The Hunt Museum provides a unique blend of art and history, making it a must-visit destination for enthusiasts seeking a rich cultural experience in the heart of Limerick.

The National Gallery of Ireland, Dublin:

Located in the heart of Dublin, the National Gallery of Ireland is a cultural hub that boasts an extensive collection of European paintings. The gallery's impressive holdings range from the Middle Ages to the modern era, featuring masterpieces by artists like

Caravaggio, Vermeer, and Rembrandt.
Irish art is also prominently featured,
with works by iconic painters such as
Jack B. Yeats. The National Gallery
plays a crucial role in promoting artistic
appreciation and education, making it
an essential stop for art lovers seeking to
explore the depth and breadth of
European and Irish art.

The Glucksman, Cork:

Tucked within the University College
Cork's scenic grounds, The Glucksman is
a contemporary art gallery that
seamlessly integrates with its natural
surroundings. The award-winning

building houses a dynamic range of exhibitions, featuring both national and international contemporary artists. The Glucksman places a strong emphasis on interdisciplinary collaboration, hosting events that bridge the worlds of art, science, and philosophy. With its ever-evolving program and commitment to fostering creative dialogue, The Glucksman contributes significantly to Cork's reputation as a vibrant center for contemporary art and cultural exchange.

The Titanic Belfast, Belfast:

As a city with a rich maritime history, Belfast is home to the Titanic Belfast, an immersive museum located on the site where the iconic RMS Titanic was built. The museum offers a poignant journey through the ship's construction, tragic sinking, and the social and cultural context of early 20th-century Belfast. Through interactive exhibits, artifacts, and audio-visual presentations, visitors gain insight into the lives of the people involved in the Titanic's story. The architectural marvel of the museum, shaped like the ship's prows, adds to the overall experience, making Titanic Belfast a compelling destination for history enthusiasts and those intrigued by the enduring legacy of the Titanic.

The Highlanes Gallery, Drogheda:

Situated in the historic town of Drogheda, the Highlanes Gallery is a contemporary art space housed in a former Franciscan church. The gallery's innovative programming showcases a diverse range of contemporary visual arts, including painting, sculpture, and photography. The emphasis on engaging with the local community is evident through educational programs and outreach initiatives. The Highlanes Gallery serves as a cultural focal point in Drogheda, bridging the gap between tradition and modernity and offering a space for both established and emerging artists to display their work.

Traditional Irish Music and Dance

The enchanting world of traditional Irish music and dance lies in the heart of Ireland's storied landscapes, transcending time with a rhythmic pulse. These artistic expressions narrate tales of love, resilience, and joy rooted in centuries of history and culture. From the haunting melodies sweeping through emerald valleys to the spirited footwork resonating in lively pub sessions, Irish music and dance embody the soul of a nation. This journey explores the origins, evolutions, and global impact of these timeless traditions, inviting you to step into the captivating rhythm that has won over the hearts of generations.

The Cliffs of Moher

Located on the rugged western coast of Ireland, the Cliffs of Moher serve not only as a breathtaking natural wonder but also as a muse for traditional Irish music. As the Atlantic waves crash against the cliffs, musicians find inspiration in the raw beauty of the landscape. Local sessions in nearby villages, such as Doolin, are renowned for their spontaneous gatherings where fiddles, tin whistles, and bodhráns create an improvised symphony. The music here resonates with the power of the sea and the resilience of the people who have called this stunning coastline home for generations.

The Sean-Nós Dance of Connemara

In the Connemara region of County Galway, the ancient art of Sean-Nós dance weaves a tapestry of intricate footwork and expressive storytelling. Rooted in the Gaelic tradition, Sean-Nós is characterized by close-to-the-floor footwork, allowing the dancer to interpret and improvise with the music. The dance is an intimate conversation between the dancer and the musician, with each step telling a story that reflects the rich history and daily lives of the Connemara people. Often performed solo, Sean-Nós dance captures the essence of a bygone era, providing a glimpse into the soul of Ireland's cultural heritage.

The Piping Tradition of County Clare

County Clare, a stronghold of traditional Irish music, has nurtured a distinctive piping tradition that has influenced generations of musicians. The haunting strains of the Uilleann pipes, an Irish bagpipe variant, and the melodic tones of the concertina resonate through the pubs and villages of the county. The rich tradition of piping competitions, such as the Willie Clancy Summer School in

Miltown Malbay, ensures the passing down of intricate tunes and techniques. The music of County Clare is a testament to the enduring legacy of Irish pipers, breathing life into melodies that have echoed through the centuries.

The Ceilidh

The Ceilidh, a communal celebration of music and dance, encapsulates the essence of traditional Irish social gatherings. Whether in a rustic village hall or a lively pub, the Ceilidh brings people together in the spirit of joyous camaraderie. Musicians strike up lively reels, jigs, and hornpipes, while dancers of all ages join in synchronized steps, creating a whirlwind of movement and laughter. The Ceilidh is a living embodiment of the interconnectedness of Irish communities, where the collective rhythm of the music and dance fosters a sense of unity and shared heritage.

The Donegal Fiddle Tradition

In the northern reaches of Ireland, the Donegal fiddle tradition holds a special place in the country's musical landscape. Famed for its distinctive ornamentation and bowing styles, the Donegal fiddle tradition has produced virtuosos like Tommy Peoples and Mairead Ní Mhaonaigh. The tunes often reflect the rugged beauty of the Donegal landscape, with melodies that echo the windswept moors and mist-covered mountains. Fiddle players in this tradition are revered for their ability to convey emotion through their music, creating a visceral connection between the listener and the raw, natural beauty of Donegal.

The Galway Flute and Whistle Tradition

Galway, a city on Ireland's west coast, has long been a hub for artistic expression. The Galway flute and whistle tradition, characterized by its vibrant ornamentation and rapid melodies, has produced musicians of international acclaim. Famed players like Matt Molloy of The Chieftains have elevated the simple tin whistle to an instrument of profound expressiveness. The lively tunes, often played in sessions along Quay Street or in cozy pub corners, showcase the city's dynamic spirit and commitment to musical innovation while staying true to the roots of traditional Irish music.

Set Dancing in Kerry

In the picturesque County Kerry, set dancing thrives as a cherished tradition. Rooted in the 19th-century quadrilles, set dances are characterized by structured patterns and precise footwork. Local halls, with polished wooden floors, come alive with the sound of fiddles, accordions, and rhythmic feet. The intricate formations of set dancing represent a communal preservation of historical dance patterns. Whether at a festival or a local gathering, Kerry's set dancing serves as a reminder of Ireland's commitment to safeguarding the intricate patterns and social dances that have been cherished for generations.

The Harp Resurgence

The harp, an emblem of Ireland for centuries, is experiencing a renaissance in the contemporary traditional music scene. Emerging talents like Úna Monaghan and Michael Rooney are rediscovering and reimagining ancient melodies, breathing new life into this iconic instrument. From solo performances to collaborations with other traditional musicians, the harp's delicate tones evoke a sense of nostalgia and connect listeners to Ireland's mythical past. As the harp regains its prominence, it symbolizes a renewed appreciation for the melodic beauty that lies at the heart of Ireland's musical heritage.

Munster's Sliabh Luachra Style

The Sliabh Luachra region, spanning the borders of Cork, Kerry, and Limerick, has birthed a unique musical style characterized by its lively jigs and slides. Fueled by fiddles and accordions, the Sliabh Luachra tradition is known for its infectious rhythm and spontaneous ornamentation. Renowned musicians like Julia Clifford and Denis Murphy have left an indelible mark on the region's musical legacy. The Sliabh Luachra style, with its emphasis on close, intimate sessions, showcases the camaraderie that defines traditional Irish music, where the joy of playing and dancing is shared among friends and family.

The Burren

In the rocky expanse of County Clare lies The Burren, a unique landscape that serves as a backdrop for a distinctive musical tradition. The region's musicians, inspired by the stark beauty of their surroundings, have developed a style characterized by its intricate ornamentation and thoughtful interpretation. The Burren's traditional music sessions, often held in cozy pubs nestled within the limestone landscape, embody the harmonious blend of nature and art. Musicians in The Burren celebrate a connection to the land, and their music reflects the resilience and beauty of a region that has shaped Ireland's cultural heritage in its own unique way.

Festivals and Events

Throughout the year, Ireland hosts a variety of festivals and events that

showcase its unique charm. From lively
music festivals that celebrate the deep-
rooted musical legacy of the country to
colorful parades honoring centuries-old
traditions, Ireland offers a diverse and
dynamic calendar of events. These
festive celebrations not only unite
communities but also welcome visitors
to experience the warmth and
hospitality that define the Irish spirit.

St. Patrick's Day Festival: A Sea of Green in Dublin

St. Patrick's Day is an annual celebration of Ireland's patron saint, St. Patrick, known for bringing Christianity to the island. The festival, observed on March 17th, commemorates his death with a cultural extravaganza. In Dublin, the festivities center around a lively parade, featuring traditional Irish music, dance, and vibrant displays of national pride. The green theme symbolizes the lush landscapes of Ireland and has become synonymous with the global celebration of Irish culture.

Fleadh Cheoil: A Musical Extravaganza for All Ages

Fleadh Cheoil, meaning "festival of music" in Irish, is an event rooted in the country's deep musical heritage. Originating in the early 20th century, the festival aims to preserve and promote traditional Irish music. Its dynamic program includes competitions, workshops, and spontaneous sessions, fostering a sense of community among musicians and enthusiasts. The event rotates among different towns, ensuring widespread participation and spotlighting diverse local traditions.

Galway International Arts Festival: Where Arts and Culture Converge

Founded in 1978, the Galway International Arts Festival has evolved into one of Europe's foremost cultural celebrations. This multi-disciplinary event brings together artists from various backgrounds, showcasing the best in theater, visual arts, dance, and music. The festival transforms Galway into a vibrant cultural hub, attracting both local and international audiences to immerse themselves in the creative tapestry that defines contemporary Irish art.

Belfast International Arts Festival: A Cultural Showcase in the North

The Belfast International Arts Festival, established in 1962, emerged during a time of cultural resurgence in Northern Ireland. The festival plays a pivotal role in promoting inclusivity and diversity, providing a platform for both local and international artists. By offering a diverse range of artistic expressions, from traditional Irish to cutting-edge global performances, the festival contributes significantly to Belfast's cultural renaissance and showcases the city's commitment to the arts.

Dublin Horse Show: Equestrian Elegance in the Capital

The Dublin Horse Show has been a highlight of Ireland's equestrian calendar since its inception in 1868. Held at the Royal Dublin Society (RDS), the event initially focused on showcasing the country's best horses. Over the years, it evolved into a comprehensive equestrian spectacle, featuring world-class show jumping competitions, trade displays, and family-friendly activities.

The Dublin Horse Show is a testament to Ireland's deep-rooted connection with horses and its rich equestrian tradition.

Electric Picnic: Ireland's Premier Music and Arts Festival

Since its inception in 2004, Electric Picnic has grown to become Ireland's premier music and arts festival. Set against the backdrop of Stradbally Estate, the festival aims to create a utopian escape where diverse artistic expressions converge. The event has earned a reputation for its eclectic lineup, encompassing mainstream and niche genres, as well as its commitment to promoting sustainability and a vibrant, inclusive atmosphere.

Listowel Writers' Week: A Literary Feast in Kerry

Listowel Writers' Week, inaugurated in 1970, is a literary festival that brings together established and emerging writers. Nestled in County Kerry's scenic surroundings, the festival offers a unique platform for authors to engage in workshops, readings, and discussions. Inspired by the literary legacy of Listowel, the event fosters a love for literature and serves as a nurturing ground for aspiring writers to connect with established literary figures.

Dublin Theatre Festival: Spotlight on Theatrical Excellence

The Dublin Theatre Festival, founded in 1957, is one of the oldest dedicated theatre festivals in the world. It has played a pivotal role in shaping Ireland's theatrical landscape. The festival's diverse program, spanning classic and contemporary productions, attracts theater enthusiasts and artists alike. It serves as a platform for both Irish and international theater, contributing to

Dublin's reputation as a global hub for dramatic arts.

National Ploughing Championships: A Rural Spectacle

Originating in 1931, the National Ploughing Championships began as a competition to showcase the skills of Irish farmers. Over the years, it has evolved into Europe's largest outdoor exhibition, drawing farmers and spectators from across Ireland. The event celebrates Ireland's rural heritage, featuring ploughing competitions, modern agricultural machinery displays, and a lively trade show, making it a significant gathering for those connected to the country's agricultural roots.

Puck Fair: A Unique Animal-Focused Celebration

Puck Fair, held in the small town of Killorglin, County Kerry, has roots dating back over 400 years. The festival's centerpiece is the crowning of a wild mountain goat as "King Puck," symbolizing a blend of ancient traditions and local folklore. The event includes livestock fairs, music, and festivities, creating a distinctive celebration where the quirky charm of Ireland's cultural heritage takes center stage. Puck Fair stands as a testament to the resilience of age-old customs in modern times.

Chapter 4: Flavors of the Emerald Isle

Irish cuisine is a delightful fusion of tradition, innovation, and a profound connection to the lush landscapes that define the Emerald Isle. Renowned for its hearty and wholesome nature, Irish food reflects a rich history shaped by agricultural abundance and maritime influences. From succulent lamb stews to the iconic Irish soda bread, each dish tells a story of resilience and resourcefulness. Contemporary chefs are blending time-honored recipes with modern twists, creating a vibrant culinary scene that celebrates local produce and global influences.

Irish Cuisine

1. Soda Bread:

Originating from humble Irish kitchens, Soda Bread is a rustic and quick-to-make delight. Its history traces back to the 19th century, a time when bicarbonate of soda became a staple leavening agent. This unleavened bread, with a dense texture and slightly sweet taste, is crafted from just four basic ingredients: flour, baking soda, salt, and buttermilk. The resulting hearty loaf, often adorned with a cross to ward off evil spirits, boasts a crusty exterior and a soft, crumbly interior, making it a quintessential accompaniment to Irish meals.

2. Shellfish:

Ireland's extensive coastline has bestowed upon its cuisine a bounty of exquisite shellfish, defining its coastal gastronomy. From succulent Dublin Bay prawns to plump native oysters, the variety is as rich as the maritime history itself. These delicacies are celebrated in dishes like seafood chowder, where the briny sweetness of shellfish harmonizes with creamy broth, potatoes, and aromatic herbs. Whether grilled, steamed, or nestled in a seafood pie,

Irish shellfish captivates with its freshness and marine essence, reflecting the island's close connection to the sea.

3. Irish Stew:

A cherished emblem of Irish comfort food, Irish Stew has sustained generations with its hearty warmth. Originating from humble, rural kitchens, this one-pot wonder traditionally combines lamb, potatoes, onions, and a medley of root vegetables.

Slow-cooked to tender perfection, the stew captures the essence of Irish terroir. The marriage of earthy flavors and the succulence of slow-cooked lamb creates a wholesome, soul-satisfying dish. Seasoned with herbs like thyme and parsley, Irish Stew pays homage to Ireland's agricultural heritage, providing both sustenance and a taste of familial tradition.

4. Colcannon and Champ:

Colcannon and Champ, two beloved potato dishes, epitomize the Irish love affair with spuds. Colcannon, a hearty mash enriched with kale or cabbage, brings a textural and flavorful harmony to the humble potato. Meanwhile, Champ, a creamy amalgamation of mashed potatoes and spring onions, offers a delightful twist. Both dishes showcase the versatility of the potato, a crop deeply ingrained in Ireland's agricultural history. With a buttery richness and a touch of green freshness, these comforting classics serve as culinary canvases for celebrating the beloved Irish potato.

5. Boxty:

Hailing from the northern regions of Ireland, Boxty is a versatile potato pancake that combines grated and mashed potatoes, flour, and buttermilk. This traditional dish, with a texture reminiscent of both hash browns and traditional pancakes, offers a delightful interplay of crispy edges and a soft, doughy center. Often griddled or pan-fried to golden perfection, Boxty adapts to various accompaniments, from savory fillings like bacon and eggs to sweet toppings like sugar or fruit compote. Boxty's simplicity and adaptability make it a cherished part of Irish cuisine, representing the resourcefulness of generations past.

6. Boiled Bacon and Cabbage:

A staple of Irish home cooking, Boiled Bacon and Cabbage showcases simplicity at its best. Rooted in rural traditions, this dish features boiled pork, often cured or smoked, accompanied by cabbage, potatoes, and a peppery white sauce. The dish reflects Ireland's agricultural heritage, utilizing readily available ingredients to create a wholesome, satisfying meal. The succulent bacon, tender cabbage, and buttery potatoes meld into a harmonious ensemble, offering a taste of the countryside and the enduring appeal of uncomplicated, time-honored flavors.

7. Smoked Salmon:

Ireland's pristine waters and a legacy of skilled fishmongers contribute to the excellence of Irish Smoked Salmon. Sourced from the cold Atlantic, salmon is carefully cured and cold-smoked to achieve a delicate balance of flavors. The result is a silky, velvety texture and a rich, smoky taste that captivates the palate. Often served with traditional brown bread, capers, and a squeeze of lemon, Irish Smoked Salmon embodies the union of craftsmanship and natural abundance. Its luxurious profile makes it a timeless Irish delicacy, celebrated for both its purity and the mastery behind its preparation.

8. Black and White Pudding:

Black and White Pudding, a distinctive pair in Irish cuisine, showcase the nation's appreciation for inventive butchery and resourceful cooking. Black Pudding, made with blood, oatmeal, and spices, delivers a savory richness and a distinctive depth of flavor.

Contrastingly, White Pudding, omitting blood and incorporating suet or fat, presents a milder, lighter alternative. Both puddings, often sliced and pan-fried, contribute to traditional Irish breakfasts or find their way into various dishes, adding a unique and savory element. Their historical roots and robust flavors underscore the Irish culinary tapestry.

9. Coddle:

Coddle, a comforting and flavorsome dish, originated in Dublin as a thrifty way to use leftovers. Comprising pork sausages, bacon, onions, and potatoes, this one-pot wonder is slow-cooked to meld flavors and textures. The name "coddle" itself hints at the gentle simmering that characterizes the dish. With a savory broth infusing the ingredients, Coddle captures the essence of home-cooked warmth and communal dining. Its simple yet satisfying amalgamation of flavors reflects the Irish penchant for making the most of humble ingredients, transforming them into a culinary legacy that stands the test of time.

10. Barmbrack:

Barmbrack, a traditional Irish fruitcake, holds a place of honor in celebrations and tea times. Infused with dried fruits, such as raisins and sultanas, the sweet bread is often steeped in tea, adding depth and moisture. The name "barm" refers to the fermented yeast used in older recipes, contributing to the bread's rich flavor and airy texture. Barmbrack is steeped in superstition, as hidden charms or tokens are sometimes baked into the cake, foretelling the recipient's fortune. Whether enjoyed with a smear of butter or as part of festive gatherings, Barmbrack is a sweet embodiment of Irish hospitality and timeless traditions.

Best Restaurants

The Woollen Mills Eating House, Dublin:

The Woollen Mills Eating House exudes historic charm and culinary excellence. Housed in a building dating back to 1823, this eatery seamlessly blends tradition with modern flair. Guests can savor classic Irish dishes like Goatsbridge Farm Trout fillet with tender-stem broccoli, roasted garlic mash, and saffron cream or Feighcullen chicken with honey-roasted parsnips, cranberry relish, stuffing, and our own gravy, skillfully prepared with a contemporary twist. With its inviting atmosphere and views of the iconic Ha'penny Bridge, The Woollen Mills is a testament to Dublin's rich culinary heritage.

Kai Café + Restaurant, Galway:

In the vibrant city of Galway, Kai Café + Restaurant stands out as a beacon of farm-to-table brilliance. Chef Jess Murphy's innovative approach to Irish cuisine has earned Kai numerous accolades. The menu, a celebration of locally sourced ingredients, features dishes like aramasalata, Crudites, Crisps, Lunasa Charcuterie, Fennel Marmalade, Gubeen, Fior De Latte, Walnuts, Asparagus, Castlefranco. The cozy atmosphere and commitment to sustainable dining make Kai a must-visit for those seeking an authentic taste of Galway's culinary scene.

Farmgate Café, Cork:
Overlooking the historic English Market in Cork, Farmgate Café is a haven for food enthusiasts. This charming spot

seamlessly integrates Irish ingredients into their menu, offering delightful creations such as Cork Whiskey Cake and Irish Lambs Stew. With its commitment to showcasing the best of local produce, Farmgate Café provides a warm and inviting space for patrons to indulge in the flavors of County Cork.

An Port Mór, County Mayo:
Nestled in the scenic surroundings of County Mayo, Port Mór is a culinary gem known for its commitment to showcasing the region's bounty. Traditional Irish fare takes center stage, with standout dishes like Grilled Clew

Bay Scallops, Jerusalem Artichoke Puree, Beurre Noisette and Breast of West Cork Duck, Sweet Potato puree, and Apple Sauce. The restaurant's warm ambiance and dedication to preserving local flavors make An Port Mór a captivating stop for those exploring the culinary landscape of the West of Ireland.

1826 Adare, County Limerick

In the picturesque village of Adare, 1826 Adare is a gastronomic haven that marries modern culinary techniques with traditional Irish flavors. Renowned for its elegant setting and impeccable service, the restaurant offers dishes such as Chargrilled Prime Sirloin and Pan Fried Black Sole "on the bone". A dining experience at 1826 Adare is a journey through contemporary Irish cuisine, where each plate is a work of art.

Gregan's Castle, Ballyvaughan, County Clare

Set against the stunning backdrop of the Burren, Gregan's Castle in Ballyvaughan is an enchanting destination for food enthusiasts. The restaurant's menu, inspired by the surrounding landscapes, features dishes like Burren Smoked

Salmon and Clare Island Organic Salmon. With its commitment to sustainability and a warm, welcoming atmosphere, Gregan's Castle encapsulates the essence of County Clare's culinary prowess.

Mourne Seafood Bar, Belfast

In the heart of Belfast, Mourne Seafood Bar is a haven for seafood aficionados. Known for its fresh and locally sourced catches, the menu boasts dishes like Mussels in Garlic Cream and Fisherman's Pie. The lively ambiance and the restaurant's dedication to quality make Mourne Seafood Bar a standout choice for those seeking the best of Northern Irish seafood.

Newforge Dining Room, County Armagh

A hidden gem in County Armagh, the Newforge Dining Room is a culinary retreat steeped in history. Set within a charming Georgian country house, the restaurant offers a refined dining experience with dishes like Roast Fermanagh Sirloin and Armagh Bramley Apple Crumble. The intimate setting and emphasis on locally sourced ingredients make Newforge Dining Room a destination for those seeking an elevated taste of Armagh's culinary heritage.

The Brewer's House, Dungannon, County Tyrone:

In the heart of County Tyrone, The Brewer's House is a gastro-pub that combines traditional Irish hospitality with a contemporary culinary approach. With a menu featuring dishes like Chicken liver parfait and Gin bramble cured salmon, this establishment celebrates the rich flavors of the region. The cozy pub atmosphere and the focus on locally produced ingredients make

The Brewer's House a delightful stop for those exploring County Tyrone's culinary offerings.

Chapter 6: Local Tips

In Chapter 6, we will be sharing insider tips about traveling in Ireland. From charming villages with ancient traditions to lesser-known destinations, we will uncover the secrets that locals keep. Get ready for a journey filled with the warm hospitality of Ireland and valuable advice to make your adventure even more exciting. This chapter focuses

on straightforward, local
recommendations to help you have an
amazing time exploring the Emerald
Isle. Let's get started!

Sightseeing Recommendations

Are you curious about the best sights to
see in Ireland? Let us take you on a
visual journey as we reveal our top
recommendations for sightseeing. Our
curated list includes hidden gems and
iconic landmarks that will make your
trip to the Emerald Isle unforgettable.

Get ready to paint your travel canvas with memorable experiences!

Hidden Gems

Loop Head Peninsula:

Tucked away in County Clare, the Loop Head Peninsula offers breathtaking coastal views without the crowds. A scenic drive along the Wild Atlantic Way leads to this hidden gem, where rugged cliffs meet the roaring Atlantic Ocean. The Loop Head Lighthouse stands proudly, providing a serene atmosphere and panoramic vistas. Visitors can explore the dramatic cliffs, stroll along secluded beaches, and savor the tranquility that defines this coastal haven.

The Burren Perfumery:

Nestled in the heart of the mystical Burren in County Clare, the Burren Perfumery is a fragrant oasis producing handmade perfumes, lotions, and creams. Surrounded by limestone landscapes, this hidden gem invites visitors to explore botanical gardens, learn about traditional perfume-making techniques, and indulge in the scents of the Irish countryside. The serene setting and artisanal approach make the Burren Perfumery a truly unique experience.

Skellig Michael (Skellig Islands): While Skellig Michael gained fame through its appearance in Star Wars, the lesser-known gem is the Skellig Islands' raw beauty and rich history. Off the coast of County Kerry, these uninhabited islands feature ancient monastic ruins and diverse birdlife. Accessible by boat, the journey itself is an adventure. Exploring the beehive huts and enjoying the unspoiled landscapes make the Skellig Islands an off-the-beaten-path destination for those seeking a blend of history and nature.

Slieve League Cliffs:

Often overshadowed by the Cliffs of Moher, Slieve League Cliffs in County Donegal are among the highest sea cliffs in Europe. Towering over the Atlantic Ocean, these majestic cliffs offer awe-inspiring views without the bustling crowds. A coastal trail allows adventurous souls to witness the cliffs from various angles, providing a more intimate and less-explored alternative to the well-trodden paths of more famous counterparts.

Glenveagh National Park – Poisoned Glen:

Glenveagh National Park in County Donegal is celebrated for its pristine landscapes, but within its boundaries lies the mystical Poisoned Glen. Surrounded by the Derryveagh Mountains, this secluded valley is shrouded in myth and beauty. A short hike unveils breathtaking vistas, with Errigal, the highest peak in Donegal, serving as a majestic backdrop. The tranquility of Poisoned Glen makes it a hidden gem within the larger tapestry of Glenveagh National Park.

The Dark Hedges – Bregagh Road:

Far from the bustling city lights, the Dark Hedges on Bregagh Road in County Antrim offer a mesmerizing natural spectacle. A tunnel of ancient beech trees creates an otherworldly atmosphere, casting shadows and light that dance through the intertwined branches. While not entirely unknown, the Dark Hedges remain a serene and hauntingly beautiful location, especially during the early morning or late evening when the crowds thin, allowing for a more intimate experience.

The Copper Coast Geopark:
Stretching along the Waterford coastline, the Copper Coast Geopark is a hidden gem for geology enthusiasts and nature lovers alike. Steeped in history and geological significance, this UNESCO Global Geopark features rugged cliffs, hidden coves, and remnants of a bygone mining industry.

Exploring the diverse landscapes and uncovering the stories imprinted in the rocks make the Copper Coast Geopark a unique and underrated destination.

The Saltee Islands:

Situated off the coast of County Wexford, the Saltee Islands are a sanctuary for wildlife enthusiasts. Accessible by boat, these unspoiled islands provide a habitat for thousands of seabirds, seals, and other marine life. The untouched beauty and the sense of isolation make the Saltee Islands a haven for those seeking a peaceful retreat surrounded by the sounds of nature.

The Marble Arch Caves:

Delving beneath the surface, the Marble Arch Caves in County Fermanagh offer an underground adventure in a mesmerizing subterranean world. A network of limestone caves reveals stunning formations, underground rivers, and intricate chambers. Guided tours lead visitors through this hidden realm, providing a unique perspective on Ireland's geological wonders.

Lough Boora Parklands:

For those seeking a blend of art, nature, and tranquility, Lough Boora Parklands in County Offaly offers a distinctive experience. Formerly a peat bog, this reclaimed landscape now features outdoor sculptures, walking and cycling trails, and serene lakes. The juxtaposition of art installations against the backdrop of the Irish Midlands creates an unexpected and captivating environment, making Lough Boora Parklands a hidden gem for those looking to explore the intersection of creativity and nature.

Scenic Routes

Have you ever considered how the choice of a scenic route can transform a simple journey into an extraordinary adventure? Beyond the practicalities of travel, these winding pathways unveil a world of breathtaking landscapes, adding an immersive layer to your trip and turning the road itself into a destination worth savoring.

Ring of Kerry:

The Ring of Kerry, a picturesque 179-kilometer circular route in County Kerry, encapsulates the essence of Ireland's natural beauty. Along the way, travelers encounter stunning coastal views, quaint villages, and emerald-green landscapes. The route includes highlights like the Gap of Dunloe and the Skellig Ring, offering an immersive journey through Ireland's southwest.

Causeway Coastal Route:

Northern Ireland's Causeway Coastal Route stretches along the rugged coastline from Belfast to Londonderry, showcasing dramatic cliffs, pristine beaches, and the iconic Giant's Causeway. The route offers breathtaking views of the Atlantic Ocean, passing through quaint villages and the enchanting Glens of Antrim, making it a must-visit for those seeking coastal splendor.

Dingle Peninsula:

The Dingle Peninsula in County Kerry is a haven for scenic drives, boasting coastal cliffs, sandy beaches, and charming villages. The Slea Head Drive, a loop around the western tip, offers unrivaled views of the Blasket Islands and the Atlantic. The diverse landscapes, including the Conor Pass, make the Dingle Peninsula a visual feast for road-trippers.

Wicklow Mountains Scenic Drive:
Known as the "Garden of Ireland," County Wicklow is home to a scenic drive through the Wicklow Mountains. The route takes you through lush valleys, past serene lakes, and offers panoramic vistas from high mountain passes. Glendalough, with its ancient monastic site, adds a historical touch to this scenic journey.

Connemara Loop:

The Connemara Loop, nestled in the west of Ireland, explores the untamed beauty of Connemara in County Galway. This looped drive encompasses rugged coastlines, expansive bogs, and the Twelve Bens mountain range. The journey takes you through quaint villages like Roundstone, providing an authentic Irish experience amid breathtaking landscapes.

Healy Pass:

Healy Pass, traversing the Beara Peninsula in County Cork and County Kerry, is a winding road that offers spectacular views of the surrounding mountains and valleys. The route takes you through a remote and rugged landscape, providing a serene escape into the heart of Ireland's southwest.

Inishowen 100:

The Inishowen 100 in County Donegal is a scenic drive that encircles the Inishowen Peninsula. From Malin Head, Ireland's northernmost point, to the historic Grianan of Aileach, the route showcases diverse landscapes, including rugged cliffs, sandy beaches, and rolling hills. The Inishowen 100 immerses travelers in the raw beauty of Ireland's northern coast.

Comeragh Drive:

County Waterford's Comeragh Drive winds through the Comeragh Mountains, unveiling panoramic views of lush valleys and shimmering lakes. The route leads to the stunning Mahon Falls and the Nire Valley, providing a peaceful and off-the-beaten-path escape into Ireland's southeastern beauty.

Achill Island Circuit:

The Achill Island Circuit, off the coast of County Mayo, offers a captivating journey through Ireland's largest island. With rugged coastal cliffs, golden beaches, and the iconic Keem Bay, this route captures the essence of the Wild Atlantic Way. The Achill Sound Bridge connects the island to the mainland, setting the stage for an unforgettable drive.

The Copper Coast:

The Copper Coast, stretching along the Waterford coastline, is a UNESCO Global Geopark featuring a scenic coastal drive. Cliffs, coves, and remnants of copper mining history dot the landscape, creating a unique blend of natural beauty and industrial heritage. The route invites exploration of hidden gems along the coast, making it an ideal destination for those seeking both scenic views and historical intrigue.

Unique Experiences

Ireland, with its rich tapestry of history, culture, and landscapes, offers travelers a plethora of unique experiences that go beyond the ordinary. From mystical sites to vibrant traditions, the country is a treasure trove of unforgettable moments. Here are some exceptional and offbeat experiences that make Ireland a truly distinctive destination.

Cliffside Yoga at Cliffs of Moher:

Elevate your yoga practice to new heights at the iconic Cliffs of Moher. Imagine striking a warrior pose while overlooking the dramatic cliffs and the vast expanse of the Atlantic Ocean. Several tour operators offer sunrise or sunset yoga sessions, providing a serene and awe-inspiring setting for a truly unique wellness experience.

Falconry in Ashford Castle:

Step into the enchanting world of falconry at Ashford Castle in County Mayo. With a backdrop of the castle's grandeur, guests can partake in a hands-on falconry experience, where majestic birds of prey gracefully soar above. This immersive encounter allows for a deep connection with these incredible creatures while exploring the historic grounds of one of Ireland's most luxurious estates.

Trad on the Prom in Galway:
Dive into the heart of Irish culture with "Trad on the Prom" in Galway. This theatrical performance combines

traditional Irish music, dance, and storytelling, providing a vibrant and immersive experience. The passionate performances showcase the depth of Ireland's artistic heritage, making it an unforgettable evening filled with rhythm, energy, and storytelling.

Bog Snorkeling in County Monaghan:

For the adventurous at heart, bog snorkeling in County Monaghan offers a quirky and exhilarating experience. Competitors don snorkels and flippers to navigate a water-filled trench cut through a peat bog. This annual event attracts participants from around the world, adding a touch of whimsy to Ireland's adventurous spirit.

Stargazing in Mayo Dark Sky Park:
Discover the magic of the night sky at Mayo Dark Sky Park, one of the few Gold Tier International Dark Sky Reserves. With minimal light pollution, this pristine location provides a perfect canvas for stargazing. Join a guided astronomy tour to marvel at constellations, planets, and even the elusive Milky Way, offering a celestial experience that transcends the ordinary.

Tea Tasting at Dublin's Vintage Tea Tours:

Board a meticulously restored vintage double-decker bus in Dublin for a tea-tasting journey like no other. Dublin's Vintage Tea Tours offer a delightful blend of Irish tea, scrumptious pastries, and panoramic views of the city's landmarks. This whimsical experience combines the charm of a bygone era with the modern pleasures of a culinary adventure.

Gaelic Games Experience:

Immerse yourself in Ireland's sporting heritage with a Gaelic Games experience. Learn the intricacies of traditional Irish sports like hurling and Gaelic football through hands-on sessions with skilled instructors. Whether you're a sports enthusiast or a novice, this interactive encounter provides insight into the passion and athleticism embedded in Ireland's cultural DNA.

Sea Stack Climbing in Donegal:
For those seeking an adrenaline rush amidst stunning coastal landscapes, sea stack climbing in Donegal is a thrilling option. Scale towering sea stacks rising from the Atlantic, with the backdrop of

rugged cliffs and crashing waves. Guided by experienced instructors, this adventure offers a unique perspective of Ireland's wild and untamed coastline.

Hidden Pubs and Literary Trails in Dublin:

Explore Dublin's rich literary history by uncovering hidden pubs frequented by renowned writers. Join a literary pub crawl to discover the haunts of James Joyce, Samuel Beckett, and other literary giants. Immerse yourself in the stories and anecdotes that shaped Ireland's literary legacy, creating a connection between the present and the literary past.

Skibbereen Eagle Brewery Tour:

Delve into the world of craft beer at Skibbereen Eagle Brewery in County Cork. This microbrewery tour not only introduces visitors to the art of brewing but also offers a taste of unique and locally inspired beers. Engage with passionate brewers, savor distinctive flavors, and gain a newfound appreciation for Ireland's evolving craft beer scene.

Interaction with Locals

One of the most enriching aspects of a visit to Ireland is the opportunity for genuine interactions with its warm and welcoming locals. The Irish, renowned for their friendliness and storytelling prowess, create an authentic and memorable experience for travelers. In traditional pubs, particularly in smaller towns and villages, visitors often find themselves engaged in lively conversations with locals, sharing laughter and tales over a pint of Guinness or a cup of tea.

Beyond the pubs, exploring local markets, attending community events, or participating in cultural activities opens doors to deeper connections. Whether it's joining a traditional music session, attending a local festival, or striking up a conversation with artisans at a craft fair, these interactions provide a glimpse into the heart of Irish hospitality.

Many locals are eager to share insights into their heritage, recommend hidden gems off the tourist trail, and offer a warm invitation to experience Irish culture firsthand. These personal connections not only enhance the travel experience but also create lasting memories, leaving visitors with a sense of the genuine warmth and camaraderie that defines Ireland's spirit.

Activities and Adventures

Ireland's diverse landscapes, from rugged coastlines to lush green valleys, provide an ideal playground for a wide range of outdoor pursuits and adventures. Whether you're seeking an adrenaline rush or a more relaxed outdoor experience, the Emerald Isle offers activities that cater to every adventurer's taste.

Outdoor Pursuits

Cycling:

With its rolling hills and picturesque countryside, Ireland is a haven for cyclists. The Great Western Greenway in County Mayo is a dedicated cycling trail that stretches along the scenic west coast, while the Waterford Greenway provides a delightful ride through historic landscapes. Adventurous mountain bikers can explore purpose-built trails, such as those in Ballyhoura and Ticknock.

Rock Climbing:

For those with a passion for heights, Ireland offers excellent rock climbing opportunities. The sea cliffs of County Donegal, such as Malin Beg and Fair Head, challenge climbers with their vertical faces and stunning views. The Burren in County Clare also provides unique limestone rock formations for both beginner and experienced climbers.

Zip-lining and High Ropes Courses:

Adventure parks scattered across Ireland offer thrilling zip-lining experiences and high ropes courses. The Lough Key Forest Park in County Roscommon features an exhilarating zip-lining course, while Zipit Forest Adventures in Dublin and Cork challenge participants to navigate treetop obstacles with stunning forest backdrops.

Horseback Riding:

Embrace the romance of Ireland's landscapes on horseback, exploring scenic trails and historic sites. The Connemara region is particularly renowned for its pony trekking adventures, allowing riders to traverse the rugged terrain and pristine beaches. Equestrian centers across the country cater to riders of all skill levels, providing a unique way to connect with the Irish countryside.

Golf:

Ireland's emerald fairways are a paradise for golf enthusiasts, with renowned courses that blend challenging play with breathtaking scenery. The dramatic cliffs of Old Head Golf Links in County Cork and the traditional links courses of Ballybunion in County Kerry attract golfers from around the world, providing an unforgettable combination of sport and natural beauty.

Fishing:

Ireland's rivers and lakes are teeming with salmon, trout, and coarse fish, making it a haven for anglers. The River Shannon, Lough Corrib, and the Munster Blackwater are among the prime fishing locations. Fly fishing, coarse fishing, and sea angling opportunities abound, offering a peaceful and rewarding experience for both beginners and seasoned anglers.

Paragliding and Hang Gliding:
Soar through the skies and experience Ireland's landscapes from a new perspective with paragliding and hang gliding. The Ring of Kerry and the

Dingle Peninsula provide stunning coastal views for those seeking a thrilling airborne adventure. Skilled instructors and tandem flights cater to both novices and experienced flyers.

Camping and Wilderness Survival:
Unleash your inner adventurer with camping and wilderness survival experiences in Ireland's scenic outdoors. National parks like Glenveagh in County Donegal and Killarney in County Kerry offer designated camping areas, allowing visitors to immerse themselves in nature. Survival skills courses, such as bushcraft and wild camping, provide a

unique way to connect with the natural environment.

Bird Watching:

Ireland's diverse habitats, including coastal areas, wetlands, and mountains, make it a haven for birdwatchers. The Cliffs of Moher are home to a variety of seabirds, while the Shannon Estuary is a significant site for wintering waterfowl. Birdwatching tours and reserves across the country offer opportunities to spot rare and migratory species.

Orienteering and Geocaching:

Engage your sense of adventure with orienteering and geocaching, activities that combine navigation skills with exploration. Orienteering events take place in forests and parks, challenging participants to find checkpoints using a map and compass. Geocaching, a modern treasure hunt using GPS devices, invites explorers to discover hidden caches in both urban and rural settings.

Water Activities

Ireland's abundant coastline, inland lakes, and rivers offer a playground for water enthusiasts seeking a variety of thrilling and refreshing activities. From the crashing waves of the Atlantic to the serene waters of inland lakes, the country provides a diverse range of water adventures for every level of experience.

Surfing:

Ireland's rugged west coast is a mecca for surfers, attracting wave riders from around the globe. Destinations like

Lahinch in County Clare, Bundoran in County Donegal, and Strandhill in County Sligo boast world-class surf breaks. Whether you're a seasoned pro or a novice catching your first wave, the Atlantic swells provide an exhilarating surfing experience.

Kayaking and Canoeing:

Ireland's rivers and lakes provide ideal conditions for kayaking and canoeing adventures. Paddle through the peaceful waters of Lakes of Killarney or explore the River Boyne's historical sites. The exhilarating white-water rapids of the

River Shannon in County Limerick offer a more adrenaline-fueled experience for those seeking a thrilling aquatic escapade.

Sailing:

With its intricate network of lakes and coastal waters, Ireland is a sailor's paradise. The sheltered harbors of Cork and Galway, as well as the expansive Lough Neagh, offer excellent sailing conditions. Sailboat rentals and guided tours cater to all levels of expertise, allowing visitors to enjoy the freedom of the open water.

Windsurfing:

The windy conditions along the coasts make Ireland an excellent destination for windsurfing enthusiasts. The wide sandy beaches of Brandon Bay in County Kerry and Achill Island in County Mayo provide ideal spots for catching the wind and riding the waves. Windsurfing schools offer lessons for beginners and equipment rentals for seasoned surfers.

Sea Fishing:

For those with a passion for angling, Ireland's seas are teeming with a variety of fish. Charter boats depart from coastal towns like Kinsale and Dingle, offering deep-sea fishing adventures. Anglers can reel in everything from mackerel to sharks, providing a rewarding and memorable experience on the open sea.

Scuba Diving:

Ireland's underwater world is a hidden gem for scuba diving enthusiasts. The clear waters of the Wild Atlantic Way, particularly around the Skellig Islands and the Aran Islands, reveal vibrant marine life and submerged caves. Diving centers along the coast provide certification courses and guided dives for all skill levels.

Hiking and Walking Trails

Ireland's lush landscapes and varied terrains make it a haven for hiking and walking enthusiasts. From coastal cliffs to mountain ranges, the country boasts an extensive network of trails that cater to all levels of hikers.

Coastal Wonders along the Wild Atlantic Way:

Ireland's renowned Wild Atlantic Way boasts captivating coastal trails, each a gem in its own right. The Cliffs of Moher Coastal Walk and the Sliabh Liag Cliffs offer hikers panoramic views of the Atlantic, creating a memorable journey along the rugged western shoreline.

Peaks and Challenges in the Mourne Mountains:

For seasoned trekkers, the Mourne Mountains in Northern Ireland present a formidable challenge. The rugged peaks and diverse terrain cater to those seeking a more demanding hiking experience, rewarding their efforts with breathtaking vistas.

Tranquil Escapes in the Wicklow Mountains:

The Wicklow Mountains, just outside of Dublin, provide a serene escape with tranquil trails suitable for all levels.

Whether it's a leisurely walk through lush greenery or a more challenging trek up its hills, Wicklow offers a diverse range of experiences close to the capital.

Enchanting Paths on the Dingle Peninsula:

The Dingle Peninsula invites hikers to explore enchanting paths, such as the Slea Head Drive. Combining cultural richness with breathtaking landscapes, this region offers a perfect blend of historical charm and natural beauty for those on foot.

Unique Beauty of Connemara:

Connemara, with its vast bogs and rolling hills, beckons hikers to explore its unique and captivating beauty. The region's trails showcase Ireland's natural diversity, providing an immersive experience for those seeking a connection with the land.

Surreal Moonscape in the Burren:
The Burren in County Clare presents a surreal moonscape, captivating hikers with its unique limestone formations. The trails through this distinctive terrain offer a one-of-a-kind walking experience, showcasing the otherworldly

beauty hidden within Ireland's landscapes.

Chapter 7:

Practical Tips

In the pursuit of memorable travel experiences, wisdom lies not just in the thrill of adventure but also in the art of practicality. Being prepared and armed with practical tips can significantly enhance your journey, ensuring a smoother and more enjoyable exploration of new landscapes and cultures. From navigating the intricacies of local customs to making the most of your resources, these practical tips serve as the compass guiding you towards a seamless and enriching travel experience. Let's delve into some essential pieces of advice that can transform your adventures into a well-rounded and fulfilling journey.

Transportation:

Exploring Ireland's picturesque landscapes often involves traversing a network of roads that wind through lush green countryside, coastal cliffs, and historic towns. To make the most of your journey, understanding the transportation options available is crucial.

Car Rentals:

Renting a car provides unparalleled freedom to explore Ireland at your own pace. Numerous international and local rental companies offer a range of vehicles, from compact cars to larger family options. Remember that driving in Ireland is on the left side of the road, and roads may be narrower in rural areas. Consider renting a GPS or using a navigation app to ease your travels.

Public Transportation:
Ireland's public transportation system, including trains and buses, offers a convenient and eco-friendly way to explore the country. Irish Rail connects major cities and towns, while Bus Éireann serves both urban and rural routes. The Leap Card, a reusable smart card, simplifies payment for buses,

trains, and trams in Dublin and other selected areas.

Tour Buses and Excursions:

For those who prefer a guided experience, tour buses and excursions are widely available. These allow you to sit back, relax, and enjoy the scenery without the responsibility of driving. Day tours to popular attractions and scenic routes are offered by various companies, providing insightful commentary along the way.

Cycling:

Embrace the charm of Ireland's landscapes on two wheels by renting a bicycle. Urban areas like Dublin and Galway have bike-sharing programs, while dedicated cycling trails wind through picturesque countryside. Cycling not only allows you to connect with the environment but also provides a unique perspective on the beauty of Ireland.

Currency and Payments:

Understanding the currency and payment methods in Ireland is essential for a smooth and stress-free travel

experience. Here's a guide to help you
navigate the financial landscape:

Currency:

The official currency of the Republic of
Ireland is the Euro (€), while Northern
Ireland, as part of the United Kingdom,
uses the British Pound (£). Ensure you
have the appropriate currency for the
region you're visiting, and consider

exchanging money before your trip or withdrawing from ATMs upon arrival.

Credit and Debit Cards:

Credit and debit cards are widely accepted in Ireland, particularly in urban areas, hotels, and larger establishments. Visa and MasterCard are commonly used, while American Express and Diners Club may be less universally accepted. Notify your bank of your travel dates to avoid any issues with card transactions.

ATMs:

ATMs, known as "cash machines" in Ireland, are prevalent and dispense Euros. Be mindful of potential fees, and choose ATMs affiliated with your bank to minimize withdrawal costs. Smaller towns and rural areas may have limited ATM access, so plan accordingly.

Contactless Payments:

Contactless payment methods, using cards or mobile devices, are increasingly popular in Ireland. Many establishments, including public transportation, accept contactless payments for added convenience. Check with your bank to ensure your card is enabled for such transactions and inquire about any potential international fees.

Currency Exchange:

While major cities have currency exchange services, rates may be more favorable at banks or ATMs. Compare rates and fees to choose the most cost-effective option. Consider exchanging a small amount for initial expenses and relying on ATMs for subsequent withdrawals.

Tipping Etiquette:

Tipping is customary in Ireland but not mandatory. In restaurants, leaving a tip of 10-15% for good service is common. Tipping for other services, such as taxi rides and hotel staff, is also appreciated but discretionary.

Mobile Payments:

Mobile payment apps, such as Apple Pay and Google Pay, are gaining popularity in Ireland. Check if your device and payment method are compatible with local establishments that support this convenient and secure way of making transactions.

Budgeting:

Plan your budget considering the cost of accommodations, meals, transportation, and attractions. Ireland, like many European destinations, may have a higher cost of living, particularly in tourist-heavy areas. Researching and setting a realistic budget will help you make the most of your trip without overspending.

Emergency Cash:

Carry a small amount of emergency cash for situations where cards may not be accepted. It's always wise to have a backup in case of unexpected circumstances.

Communication:

As you embark on your journey through Ireland, effective communication is key to immersing yourself in the rich cultural tapestry and ensuring a smooth and enjoyable experience. Here are some insights into communication norms and tips to connect with the locals:

English Language:

English is the official language in Ireland, and you'll find locals fluent in this language. However, be prepared for the distinctive Irish accent and colloquialisms, which add a charming and unique flavor to the communication.

Irish Phrases and Greetings:

While English is widely spoken, incorporating a few Irish phrases into your interactions can endear you to the locals. Common greetings like "Dia dhuit" (Hello) and "Sláinte" (Cheers) reflect an appreciation for the Irish language and culture.

Friendly and Approachable Locals:

The Irish are known for their friendliness and sociable nature. Don't hesitate to strike up conversations with locals in pubs, shops, or during your travels. The warmth of the Irish people often leads to spontaneous and enjoyable encounters.

Politeness and Respect:

Politeness and respect are highly valued in Irish culture. Using "please" and "thank you" goes a long way, and addressing people with courtesy, especially in rural areas, contributes to positive interactions.

Storytelling Tradition:

Embrace the Irish love for storytelling. Many locals enjoy sharing anecdotes, folklore, and tales of local history. Listening attentively and engaging in conversation about Ireland's rich cultural heritage can provide a deeper understanding of the places you visit.

Pubs as Social Hubs:

Pubs play a central role in Irish social life. They serve as gathering places where locals engage in conversations, share stories, and enjoy traditional music. Joining in on these experiences not only enhances your trip but also allows you to connect with the heart of Irish culture.

Weather and Clothing:

Ireland's weather is famously unpredictable, often experiencing "four seasons in one day." To make the most of your visit and stay comfortable, understanding the weather patterns and packing accordingly is essential.

Layered Clothing:

The key to coping with Ireland's variable weather is layering. Even in summer, temperatures can vary, and sudden rain showers are not uncommon. A combination of layers allows you to adapt to changing conditions, whether you're exploring coastal cliffs or strolling through quaint villages.

Waterproof Gear:

Invest in a good waterproof jacket and sturdy, water-resistant footwear. Ireland's rain showers can be brief but intense, and having reliable rain gear ensures you stay dry and comfortable during your outdoor activities.

Warm Accessories:

Even in milder seasons, evenings can be cool. A warm sweater or fleece, along with a hat and gloves, is advisable, especially if you plan to be out enjoying the evening air or attending outdoor events.

Comfortable Footwear:

Comfortable and waterproof footwear is crucial, particularly if you're planning to explore hiking trails or rural areas. Ireland's landscapes can be rugged, and suitable footwear will enhance your overall comfort and enjoyment.

Sun Protection:

Despite its reputation for rain, Ireland does experience sunny days. Pack sunscreen, sunglasses, and a hat to protect yourself from the sun's rays, especially if you're spending extended periods outdoors.

Seasonal Considerations:

Ireland experiences distinct seasons. Winters are relatively mild, but a warm coat and additional layers are advisable. Spring and autumn bring milder temperatures, while summer can be a mix of warm and cool days. Check the weather forecast before your trip to pack accordingly.

Conclusion

As you reach the conclusion of this
guide, I hope the insights and tips
provided have ignited a sense of
excitement and anticipation for the
unforgettable journey that lies ahead in
Ireland. Traveling through the Emerald
Isle is not just about exploring its scenic

landscapes, historic sites, or engaging in unique activities; it's about immersing yourself in a rich tapestry of culture, connecting with warm-hearted locals, and creating lasting memories.

Ireland beckons with an enchanting allure that transcends the ordinary, making it a destination that demands exploration. From its emerald landscapes and rugged coastlines to the warmth of its welcoming locals, Ireland is a tapestry of culture, history, and natural beauty. Immerse yourself in the spirited charm of its lively cities, discover hidden gems along scenic routes, and savor the rich traditions found in cozy pubs. Whether you're captivated by ancient castles, drawn to the haunting melodies of traditional music, or seeking solace in its serene countryside, Ireland promises an unforgettable journey filled with vibrant experiences, genuine connections, and moments that linger in the heart forever.

Embrace the unpredictability of Ireland's weather, savor the charm of its vibrant cities and quaint villages, and relish the camaraderie found in its traditional pubs. Remember that the heart of Ireland beats not just in its captivating landscapes but in the stories shared by its people, the lilt of its music, and the timeless traditions that shape its identity.

As you traverse the scenic routes, whether by car, on foot, or through the camaraderie of guided tours, let each winding road and hidden gem unfold a new chapter in your adventure. Seize every opportunity to engage with locals, listen to their stories, and perhaps share a few of your own. The Irish spirit, known for its warmth and hospitality, invites you to become a part of its narrative.

In your explorations, may you find moments of tranquility in the embrace of nature, the thrill of unexpected adventures, and the joy of connecting with a culture that celebrates life with zest. Ireland, with its ever-changing weather, timeless landscapes, and spirited people, promises an experience that transcends the ordinary.

As you embark on this journey, let the encouragement within these pages be a companion on your travels. May it inspire you to step outside your comfort zone, to relish the diversity of experiences, and to create memories that will stay etched in your heart for years to come. Your adventure in Ireland awaits—immerse yourself fully, embrace the unknown, and cherish the magic of the Emerald Isle. Safe travels, and may your trip be nothing short of unforgettable. Sláinte!

Summary

Are you ready for an amazing adventure through the heart of Ireland? Let Nicholas Vega be your guide! His meticulously crafted guide offers an unbeatable blend of ancient history, art, culture, and culinary treasures that will leave you absolutely mesmerized.

As you dive into the narrative, the guide provides a brief yet insightful overview of Ireland, setting the stage for exploring its rich heritage. And let me tell you, there's so much to explore! Vega draws on a wide range of reputable sources to unveil the country's breathtaking historical tapestry, inviting you to

227

discover ten must-visit sites in each category ranging from archaeological wonders to majestic castles and charming towns.

But that's not all! The guide masterfully immerses you in Ireland's vibrant cultural scene, exploring everything from world-class museums to traditional music and dance. And let's not forget about the incredible food! You'll be introduced to the diverse flavors of Irish cuisine, from iconic dishes such as Irish stew and soda bread to hidden gems such as boxty and coddle. Trust me, your taste buds will thank you.

And if you're looking for the best places to enjoy a pint of Guinness or a dram of Irish whiskey, the guide has got you covered. You'll also get to explore the ten best restaurants across Ireland, complete with insightful reviews and tantalizing descriptions of must-try dishes.

But wait, there's more! Nicholas Vega also shares invaluable tips for an immersive and seamless experience. You'll get sightseeing recommendations that include hidden gems and scenic routes, unique experiences, and practical advice on transportation, currency, communication, and weather. He'll help you navigate Ireland's winding roads, avoid tourist traps, and connect with locals who are eager to share their stories and traditions.

As the journey concludes, the guide recaps the highlights and encourages you to embrace the magic of Ireland. Trust me, you won't want to leave this incredible country. With Vega's guide, you're guaranteed an unforgettable trip where history, culture, and culinary delights converge in a breathtaking tapestry of experiences.

Made in the USA
Las Vegas, NV
12 July 2024

92224577R00128